the WORLD'S BEST SPORTS RiDDLES and JOKES

by
JOSEPH ROSENBLOOM
PicTuRES by Sanford HOFFMAN

Sterling Publishing Co., Inc.   New York

Copyright © 1988 by Joseph Rosenbloom
Published by Sterling Publishing Co., Inc.
Two Park Avenue, New York, N.Y. 10016
Distributed in Canada by Oak Tree Press Ltd.
% Canadian Manda Group, P.O. Box 920, Station U
Toronto, Ontario, Canada M8Z 5P9
Distributed in the United Kingdom by Blandford Press
Link House, West Street, Poole, Dorset BH15 1LL, England
Distributed in Australia by Capricorn Ltd.
P.O. Box 665, Lane Cove, NSW 2066
Manufactured in the United States of America
All rights reserved

Library of Congress Cataloging-in-Publication Data

Rosenbloom, Joseph.
  The world's best sports riddles and jokes / by Joseph Rosenbloom;
illustrated by Sanford Hoffman.
    p. cm.
  Includes index.
  Summary: Presents hundreds of riddles and jokes relating to
football, baseball, weightlifting, karate, croquet, and other
sports.
  ISBN 0-8069-6772-2. ISBN 0-8069-6773-0 (lib. bdg.)
  1. Sports—Anecdotes, facetiae, satire, etc. 2. American wit and
humor. [1. Riddles. 2. Jokes. 3. Sports—Wit and humor.]
I. Hoffman, Sanford, ill. II. Title.
PN6231.S65R58 1988   87-30434
818'.5402—dc19   CIP
                                             AC

CONTENTS

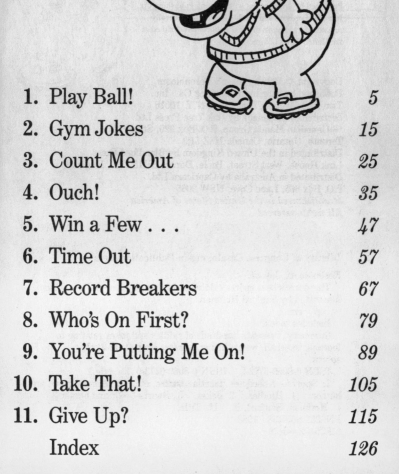

To Burton Hobson

• 1 •
PLAY BALL!

What position do pigs play on a baseball team?
Short-slop.

What is a shortstop's favorite saying?
"If at first you don't succeed, try the out-field."

What do you call a dog that stands behind home plate?
The catcher's mutt.

What was a spider doing on the baseball team?
Catching flies.

Where do coal diggers play baseball?
In the minor (miner) leagues.

Why couldn't Robin play baseball?
He forgot his bat, man.

How do you hold a bat?
By the wings.

What has two gloves and four legs?
Two baseball players.

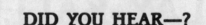

DID YOU HEAR—?

Did you hear about the baseball player who was so kind, he wouldn't even hit a fly?

What is the baseball version of "Star Wars"?
"The Umpire Strikes Back."

When is an umpire like a telephone operator?
When he makes a call.

What kind of umpires do you find at the North Pole?
Cold ones.

What is the difference between an umpire and a pickpocket?

> *The umpire watches steals, the pickpocket steals watches.*

How are tough teachers like umpires?

> *They penalize you for errors.*

Why did the umpire penalize the stale bread?

> *It tried to get fresh.*

Why did the umpire penalize the chicken?

> *For using fowl (foul) language.*

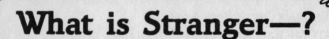

What is Stranger—?

What is stranger than seeing a shrimp roll?

Seeing a clam bake.

What is stranger than seeing a clam bake?

Seeing a bread box.

What is stranger than seeing a bread box?

Seeing a kitchen sink.

What is stranger than seeing a kitchen sink?

Seeing a bed spring.

What is stranger than seeing a bed spring?

Seeing a toilet bowl.

Why was the football coach unpopular?

He was rotten to the end.

What do you give a football player with big feet?

Large shoes.

CUSTOMER: Do you sell football shoes?
CLERK: Sure. What size is your football?

REPORTER: What position do you play in the football game?
PLAYER: Oh, sort of crouched down and bent over.

What is the difference between a football player and a duck?

You find one in the huddle, the other in a puddle.

How do football players get clean?

They use scrub teams.

How can you tell if there is a football team in your bathtub?

It is hard to close the shower curtain.

Which football player wears the biggest helmet?

The one with the biggest head.

How do you serve a football player his clam chowder?

In a soup-er bowl.

What did the football say to the player?
"I get a kick out of you."

What did the football say after the player threw it?
"You send me!"

What did the helmet say to the football player?
"You're putting me on!"

How do we know that football referees are happy?
Because they whistle while they work.

What do you call a 300-pound football player with a short temper?
"Sir."

What do you do with a blue football player?
Cheer him up.

What do you do with a green hockey player?
Teach him something.

What do you do with a green basketball player?
Wait until he ripens.

Who's the favorite poet of basketball players?
Longfellow.

What is purple and wrinkled and makes pit stops?

A racing prune.

Where do race cars go swimming?
In the car pool.

Where do ghosts go swimming?
At the sea ghost (coast).

Where do mummies go swimming?
In the Dead Sea.

What do you call two logs in the water?
A pair of swimming trunks.

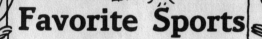

Favorite Sports

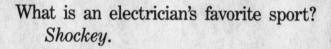

What is an electrician's favorite sport?
Shockey.

What is a mosquito's favorite sport?
Skin diving.

What is an executioner's favorite sport?
Hang gliding.

What is a frog's favorite sport?
Croquet.

What is a pig's favorite sport?
Pig-pong.

What is King Kong's favorite sport?
Ping-Kong.

What is a horse's favorite sport?
Stable tennis.

What is Lassie's favorite sport?
Collie ball.

What kind of ball games do eggs play?
Soft-boil and hard-boil.

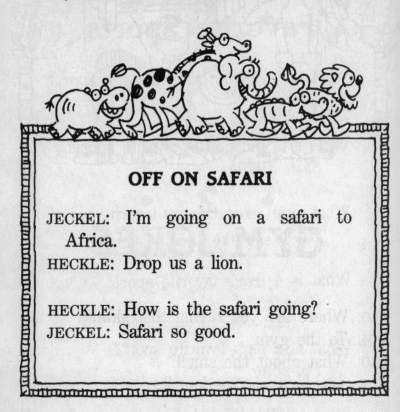

OFF ON SAFARI

JECKEL: I'm going on a safari to Africa.

HECKLE: Drop us a lion.

HECKLE: How is the safari going?

JECKEL: Safari so good.

Have you ever hunted bear?
No, but I've gone hiking in my shorts.

• 2 •
GYM JOKES

FLO: Where are you taking that skunk?
MOE: To the gym.
FLO: What about the smell?
MOE: Oh, he'll get used to it.

What kind of bell doesn't ring?
   A dumbbell.

Why did the chicken lift weights?
   She needed the eggs-ercise.

What grows on trees and can lift tremendous weights?
   Hercu-leaves.

BOXER: Feel my muscles. They're like potatoes.

TRAINER: Yes, mashed potatoes.

**That weightlifter
is so strong—**

**How strong
is he?**

He's so strong, he pitches horseshoes
without taking them off the horses.

He's so strong, that on his birthday, he
threw a party.

He's so strong, that when he sticks out
his tongue, he breaks a tooth.

SUE: Why are you taking those math questions
to Jack LaLanne?

LOU: My teacher told me to reduce some
fractions.

The weightlifting champion was always bragging about his strength. Everyone was tired of listening to him boast, but no one knew how to shut him up. Finally, a small man had an idea.

"I bet you," he said to the weightlifter, "that I can wheel something around the block in a wheelbarrow—but you can't wheel it back."

"The weightlifter looked the small man up and down and said, "I'll take that bet."

The small man smiled, gripped the handles of the wheelbarrow, and said to the weightlifter, "Hop in, please."

He then wheeled the weightlifter around the block—and won the bet.

Why were the police called to the school's basketball game?

Someone said there were a bunch of sneakers and loafers in the gym.

What do basketball players read in their spare time?

Tall stories.

How do you talk to a 7-foot-tall basketball player?

Use BIG words.

Why is it hard for basketball players to be neat?

Because they dribble so much.

Why was the termite kicked off the basketball team?

It ate the backboard.

When it was time for the college basketball team to sign up players, the coach hung a sign over the door to his office. It read:

THIS DOOR IS 6 FEET HIGH.
IF YOU CAN ENTER
WITHOUT STOOPING—DON'T!

That basketball player is so tall—

How tall is he?

He's so tall, he has to stand on a ladder to shave himself.

He's so tall, he has to get on his knees just to put his hands in his pockets.

SALLY: What is the difference between a basketball, a boxing glove and a bottle of glue?

ALLY: I don't know, what?

SALLY: A basketball is round, and a boxing glove isn't.

ALLY: But what about the bottle of glue?

SALLY: That's where you get stuck.

If a basketball team were chasing a baseball team, what time would it be?

Five after nine.

What would you get if you crossed a basketball with a newborn snake?

A bouncing baby boa.

Why did the basketball player throw the ball into the ocean?

The coach told him to sink it.

Why did the basketball players hold their noses?

Someone was about to make a foul shot.

How did the midget qualify for the basketball team?

He lied about his height.

What would you get if you cloned and froze a player on the Los Angeles Lakers?

An iced Kareem clone.

SAM: I have a chance for the soccer team.
PAM: I didn't know they were raffling it off.

Why do soccer players do well in school?

They know how to use their heads.

DID YOU HEAR—?

Did you hear about the soccer player who didn't do well in school?

He was a left back.

Did you hear about the football player who asked his coach to flood the field?

He wanted to go in as a sub.

SAL: Did you hear about the Teacher-Student football game?
HAL: Who won?
SAL: No one. The teachers were so mean, they refused to pass the ball.

Did you hear about the forward pass?
Never mind, you wouldn't catch it.

FLIP: I know a gymnast who is so flexible, she can lift her leg over her head.

FLOP: That's nothing. I know a sailor who is so flexible, he can sit on his chest.

What is brown and white and turns cartwheels?

A brown and white horse pulling a cart.

Why are Boy Scouts such great gymnasts?

They're always doing good turns.

SIGN IN GYM:

THE WORLD
IS IN BAD SHAPE—
MUST YOU BE, TOO?

The teacher was giving her first grade class a quiz on counting. Carol got things started by counting to 10.

"Now, Albert," said the teacher, "you take over by beginning with 11."

"11, 14, 23, 42, 26," said Albert.

"What kind of counting is that?" asked the teacher.

"Who's counting?" replied Albert. "I'm calling signals."

What flavor ice cream do cheerleaders like best?

Rahs-berry.

What do cheerleaders like to drink?

Root beer.

Which three R's must every cheerleader know?

"Rah! Rah! Rah!"

What color is a cheerleader?

Yeller (yellow).

What do cheerleaders have for breakfast?

Cheer-ios.

Who wears a coonskin cap and plays an English Game?

Davy Cricket.

Why did the elephant go to the gym wearing Adidas?

His Reeboks were in the wash.

Why do elephants wear blue sneakers?

Because white ones get dirty too fast.

Where did the Loch Ness monster put on its sneakers?

In the loch-er room.

What did one toad say to the other toad?

"One more game of leap frog—and I'll croak!"

What did the fencer say when he was defeated?

"Curses! Foiled again!"

What does a fencing master do at 12 o'clock?

He goes to lunge.

• 3 •
COUNT ME OUT

What happens when you hit a pop fly?
The same thing that happens when you hit a mom fly.

How do you make a fly ball?
Hit him with a bat.

What is the best way to get rid of flies?
Get good outfielders.

What is the best way to get rid of demons?
Exorcise (exercise).

How can you pitch a winning baseball game without ever throwing a ball?
Throw only strikes.

What has 18 legs and catches flies?
A baseball team.

When do monkeys play baseball?
In Ape-ril.

When does Humpty-Dumpty play baseball?
In the fall.

Why was the night baseball invented?
Because bats like to sleep during the day.

What do you get if you cover a baseball field with sandpaper?
A diamond in the rough.

Why did the golfer wear two pairs of pants?
In case he got a hole in one.

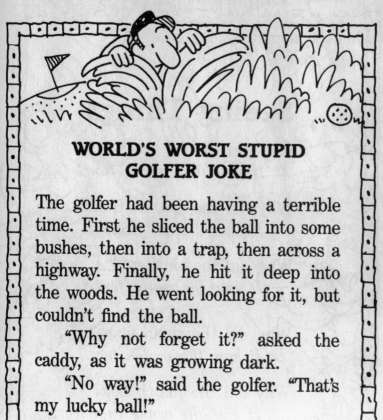

WORLD'S WORST STUPID GOLFER JOKE

The golfer had been having a terrible time. First he sliced the ball into some bushes, then into a trap, then across a highway. Finally, he hit it deep into the woods. He went looking for it, but couldn't find the ball.

"Why not forget it?" asked the caddy, as it was growing dark.

"No way!" said the golfer. "That's my lucky ball!"

Why are golf balls small and white?
Because if they were big and gray, they'd be elephants.

How do you make a golf ball float?
Take two scoops of ice cream. Add root beer. Then drop in the golf ball.

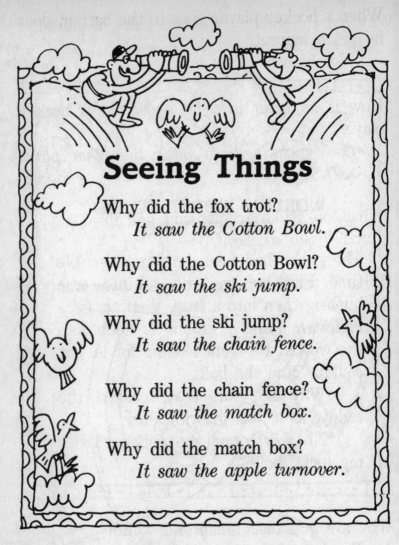

Seeing Things

Why did the fox trot?
  It saw the Cotton Bowl.

Why did the Cotton Bowl?
  It saw the ski jump.

Why did the ski jump?
  It saw the chain fence.

Why did the chain fence?
  It saw the match box.

Why did the match box?
  It saw the apple turnover.

What has two blades and breathes fire?
  A dragon on ice skates.

What position do monsters play on a hockey team?
  Ghoulie.

When a hockey player goes to the barber, does he get a haircut?

No, he gets all of them cut.

How is an actor in a hit show like a hockey player?

One sticks with a play, the other plays with a stick.

What looks like an elephant and flies?

A flying elephant.

What is the last thing a trapeze flyer wants to be?

The fall guy.

What is black and white and red all over?
A penguin that has done 100 push-ups.

DIT: One Sunday a man went swimming in the river. When he wanted to come back on shore, he couldn't.

DOT: Why not?

DIT: The banks are closed on Sunday.

What did Cinderella wear when she went to the beach?
Glass flippers.

"Did you know I was a life saver last summer?"
"Really? What flavor?"

What happened when the diver leaped 100 feet into a glass of root beer?

Nothing. It was a soft drink.

Why wouldn't the skeleton jump off the diving board?

It had no guts.

Why weren't the elephants allowed in the swimming pool?

Because they couldn't keep their trunks up.

What do you get if an elephant sucks up all the water in a swimming pool and squirts it out?

A jumbo jet.

ERNIE: Do you always swim with your socks on?

BERNIE: Only when the water is cold.

What do lawyers like to wear when they go swimming?

Bathing suits.

What do lawyers wear when they go running?

Briefs.

31

What sport is like a perfect score in the Olympics?

Tennis (ten is).

Why are waiters like tennis players?

They both have to know how to serve.

Do vampires play tennis?

No, they prefer bat-minton.

What is the difference between the Prince of Wales and a tennis ball?

One is heir to the throne, the other is thrown to the air.

What is the difference between a doughnut and a tennis racket?

You can't dunk a tennis racket in a glass of milk.

LES: My watch says it's eight-ish.
BESS: Mine says it's nine-ish.
JESS: Ten-ish, anyone?

FRED: What do you call a blond stick used in billiards?
RED: Tan cue?
FRED: You're welcome!

POLLY: I went riding today.
MOLLY: Horseback?
POLLY: Sure. It got back two hours before I did.

BETTY: I went horseback riding and got a headache.
NETTY: That's not where I ache when I go horseback riding.

What four letters can you say to someone who has been in the ring with a professional wrestler?

R-U-O-K?

Where does a big, mean, 300-pound-wrestler sit when he gets on a bus?

Anywhere he wants to.

Would you rather have a 300-pound football player attack you or a 300-pound wrestler?

I'd rather have them attack each other.

How do you tell a big, mean wrestler from a bunny rabbit?

You don't tell a big, mean wrestler anything.

Why couldn't the wrestler light the fire?

Because he lost all his matches.

What is the difference between a wrestler pinned to the mat and a rainy day?

One is roaring with pain, the other is pouring with rain.

LEN: If I arm-wrestled you, who would win?
GWEN: I give up, who?
LEN: I would. You just gave up.

• 4 •
OUCH!

What tree is a karate champion?
Spruce Lee.

What is small, round and green and knows karate?
Bruce Pea.

What sickness did Bruce Lee get every winter?
Kung Flu.

Why did the karate expert wear a black belt?
To keep his pants up.

Why did the weightlifter wear black suspenders?
To keep his shoulders down.

How do you shake hands with a judo expert?
Very carefully.

Why did the matador take judo lessons?
He wanted to learn how to throw the bull.

DID YOU HEAR—?

Did you hear about the karate expert who joined the army? The first time he saluted, he nearly killed himself.

GUS: Did you hear about the big fight at the bus station?
RUSS: No, what happened?
GUS: Two tickets got punched.

Did you hear the joke about the muscle?
Never mind, it's a lot of mush.

What do you get when a pea picks a fight with a boxer?
A black-eyed pea.

What kind of potatoes do you get when you step into the ring with the heavyweight champion of France?
French fright (fried).

Why is a boxer's hand never larger than eleven inches long?

If it were twelve inches long, it would be a foot.

What was the artist doing in the boxing ring?

They needed him in case the fight ended in a draw.

What is the difference between a winter day and a boxer who is down for the count?

One is cold out, the other is out cold.

What is the difference between a nail and a bad boxer?

One is knocked in, the other is knocked out.

What is the difference between an ice cream cone and a professional boxer?

You can lick one, the other can lick you.

On the door of a school was a sign that read:

PLEASE DON'T KNOCK
BEFORE ENTERING

What kind of school was it?

A karate school.

REPORTER: What made you take up the sport of sky diving?

PARACHUTIST: A four-engine aircraft with three dead engines.

What would you get if two outlaw gangs entered a sky diving contest?

A chute out.

What kind of flying school doesn't anyone want to go to?

One that has a crash course.

How are airplane pilots like football players?

They're both interested in safe touchdowns.

How do you shoot a basketball?
With a BB gun.

What do you call it when a duck is hit by a bullet?
A foul (fowl) shot.

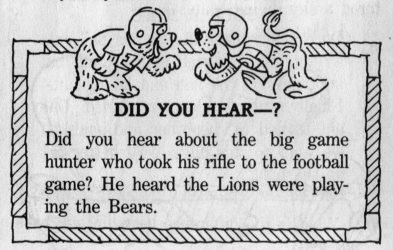

DID YOU HEAR—?

Did you hear about the big game hunter who took his rifle to the football game? He heard the Lions were playing the Bears.

FIRST HUNTER: For goodness sake, why didn't you shoot? That tiger almost got me!

SECOND HUNTER: But you told me this was an elephant gun.

Sherlock Holmes stood over the dead body of a man named Juan.

SHERLOCK: Obviously, Watson, he was killed with a golf gun.

WATSON: Really, Holmes? What's a golf gun?

SHERLOCK: It's a gun that makes a hole in Juan (a hole in one).

WORLD'S WORST TERRIBLE GOLFER JOKE

Once a terrible golfer hit his ball onto an ant hill. He tried to hit it off, but kept missing the ball and killing ants. Finally, only two ants remained. One ant turned to the other and said, "If we want to stay alive, we'd better get on the ball!"

VAL: What is the difference between golf balls and *snoo*?

CAL: What's *snoo*?

VAL: Nothing much, what's snoo with you?

What goes putt, putt, putt, putt, putt?
    A bad golfer.

What does a dog use for playing golf?
    A kennel club.

NED: Lost your job as a caddy?

TED: Yes, I could do the work all right, but I just couldn't learn not to laugh.

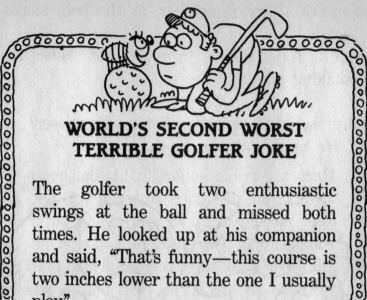

WORLD'S SECOND WORST TERRIBLE GOLFER JOKE

The golfer took two enthusiastic swings at the ball and missed both times. He looked up at his companion and said, "That's funny—this course is two inches lower than the one I usually play."

Tom and Jerry were playing golf when a bird flew overhead.

"Look at that duck," Tom said.

"That's not a duck," said Jerry. "That's a goose."

"Duck!"

"Goose!"

And so the argument went. A golfer behind them, playing the hole, yelled, "Fore!" and hit the ball.

Tom saw the ball coming and shouted, "Duck!"

Jerry shouted back, "Goose!"

B-O-I-N-G!

REFEREE: Now remember, at the bell, shake hands.

BOXER: I don't have to remember. Mine are shaking already.

Why shouldn't you hit a famous composer?
He might hit you Bach.

MANAGER (*to boxer*): When I said to show him what you're made of, I didn't mean to let him knock the stuffing out of you.

Why did the boxer hit the grandfather clock?
The clock struck first.

Why did the clock strike first?
Because it was ticked off.

When are boxers like comedians?
When they have you in stitches.

When do boxers start wearing gloves?
When it gets cold.

Which part of a boxing glove hurts the most?
The outside.

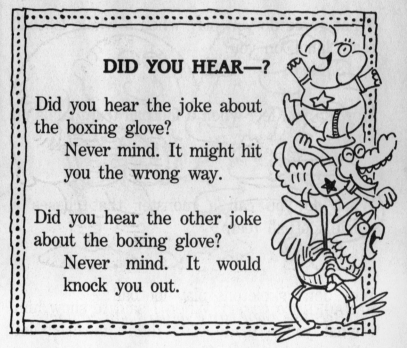

DID YOU HEAR—?

Did you hear the joke about the boxing glove?
Never mind. It might hit you the wrong way.

Did you hear the other joke about the boxing glove?
Never mind. It would knock you out.

MANAGER (*to fighter*): Don't be afraid of him. Remember, if he were any good, he wouldn't be fighting you.

The boxer was knocked out. What number did they use to revive him?
They brought him 2.

What do you call a team of really rough, tough football players?

The All-Scars.

What would you get if a whole football team landed on Batman and Robin?

Flatman and Ribbon.

What game do you play when a whole football team lands on you?

Squash.

How do you feel when a football team lands on you?

Very low.

What do you call a monster that chases a whole football team?

Hungry!

Why don't skeletons play football?

Because they can't make body contact.

MOTHER: Wesley, you've been playing football with those big boys again! You've lost your two front teeth!

WESLEY: No, I haven't, Mom. I have them in my pocket.

That football player is so tough—

**How tough
is he?**

He's so tough, he parts his hair with a chain saw.

He's so tough, he shaves with a lawn-mower.

He's so tough, he uses barbed wire for dental floss.

He's so tough, he eats beans without opening the can.

He's so tough, when he wants tea, he swallows a mouthful of water and a teabag and sits on a hot stove until the water boils.

Which side of a football is the hardest to catch?
The outside.

Why can't you play football in a small neighborhood?
Because there aren't a hundred yards in a small neighborhood.

How many feet are there in a football field?
That depends on how many people are standing in it.

What do you do when a 400-pound football player breaks his big toe?
Call a big toe (tow) truck.

Why was the tow truck driver arrested when he hitched a racing car to his truck?
They said he was trying to pull a fast one.

What happened when the racing car driver slammed into a pile of I.O.U.'s?
He ran into debt.

What are two auto racers who drive the same car?
Vroom-mates.

• 5 •
WIN A FEW . . .

How do fleas start a race?
The starter says, "One, two, flea—go!"

How do fireflies start a race?
The starter says, "Ready, set—glow!"

How do chickens start a race?
From scratch.

FLIM: My brother works out with weights.
He's so strong, this morning he tore a telephone book in half.

FLAM: That's nothing. My brother's so strong,
this morning he rushed out the door and
tore up the street.

A veteran football coach saw his championship hopes fade when, with 10 seconds left in the game and his team behind by three points, a rookie player lost the ball. The other team picked it up and scored a touchdown.

"Well," said the coach sadly, "that's the way the rookie fumbles."

What happened when the egg got nasty with the football coach?
It was egg-spelled from the game.

Why was the mayonnaise late for the game?
Because it was dressing.

A little boy knocked on the door of a friend's house. When the friend's mother answered, he said, "Can Leonard come out and play?"

"I'm afraid not," said Leonard's mother. "It's too wet and Leonard has a cold."

"Well, then," said the little boy, "can his football come out and play?"

Why didn't Cinderella get on the football team?
She had a pumpkin for a coach.

Why did Cinderella lose the game for her team?
She ran away from the ball.

What football team do ants play on?
>*The Gi-ants.*

What football team do zombies play on?
>*The Washington Deadskins.*

What can't a coach ever say to a team of zombies?
>*"Look alive!"*

TEACHER: Larry, why are you late for school?
LARRY: Well, teacher, I was dreaming about a football game, and it went into extra time—so I had to see the finish.

What does a bee wear when it goes jogging?
A swarm-up suit.

Who keeps locomotives running?
The track coach.

Where do locomotives compete?
At the track meet.

What subject do runners like best?
Jog-raphy (geography).

What is the difference between a marathon runner and a commuter?
One trains to run, the other runs to trains.

A thin man and a fat man ran a race. One ran in short bursts, the other in burst shorts.

Why did the runner race around his bed?
He wanted to catch up on his sleep.

How long should a runner's legs be?
Long enough to reach the ground.

HARRY: Did you hear about the runner who lost the marathon because of his socks?
SHARI: No—how could that be?
HARRY: They were guaranteed not to run.

Who is Count Dracula's favorite person on the baseball team?

The bat boy.

What is the difference between a baseball player and a vampire?

One bats flies, the other flies bats.

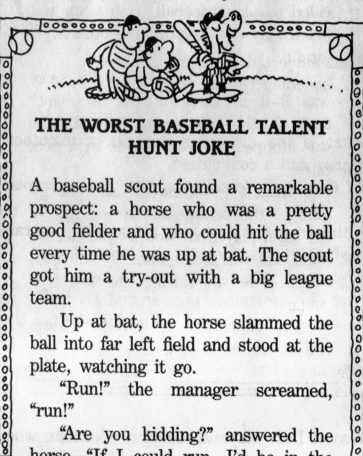

THE WORST BASEBALL TALENT HUNT JOKE

A baseball scout found a remarkable prospect: a horse who was a pretty good fielder and who could hit the ball every time he was up at bat. The scout got him a try-out with a big league team.

Up at bat, the horse slammed the ball into far left field and stood at the plate, watching it go.

"Run!" the manager screamed, "run!"

"Are you kidding?" answered the horse. "If I could run, I'd be in the Kentucky Derby."

WORLD'S WORST CENTIPEDE JOKE

Some of the animals on Noah's ark decided to play baseball. One team was headed by an elephant, the other by a giraffe.

By the fourth inning, the score was 9–0 in favor of the elephant's team. In the fifth inning, a hard drive was stopped by a centipede in a neat catch.

"What a great catch!" said the giraffe to the centipede. "If the rest of the team played as well as you do, we could still win this game! By the way, where were you during the first four innings?"

The centipede answered, "I was putting on my sneakers."

Why did the silly baseball fan take his car to the game?

He heard it was a long drive to center field.

SILLIEST BAFFLING PUZZLE JOKE

Carlos left home one night. He turned to the right and started running. He ran straight ahead. Then he turned to the left. After a while, he turned to the left again. He was running faster than ever. Then he turned left once again and headed for home. But in the distance he saw two masked men waiting for him. Who were they?

Carlos was a baseball player. He had just hit a triple and was trying to turn it into a home run. One of the masked men waiting for him at home plate was the other team's catcher. The second masked man was the umpire.

The teacher asked the class to write a composition about baseball. One minute later, Henry turned in his paper. It read, "Game called on account of rain."

What would you get if you cross a lobster and a baseball player?

A pinch hitter.

Why was the mummy sent into the game as a pinch hitter?

With a mummy at bat, the game would be all tied up.

What ghost haunts a team?

The team spirit.

Why is school like baseball?

The bell strikes one, two, three—and you're out!

What is the difference between someone who hits the ball but does not score—and someone who beats a chicken?

One fouls the hit, the other hits the fowl.

What is the difference between a queen who likes to dance and a baseball player?

One throws balls, the other catches them.

COACH: We have a great team this year. So far we have had no losses, no draws and no goals scored against us.

REPORTER: How many games have you played?

COACH: The first one is next Sunday.

DID YOU HEAR—?

Did you hear the joke about the game with the 0–0 score?
Never mind, it's pointless.

Why did the silly baseball player bring his bat to bed?

He wanted to hit the hay.

Why did the rookie player put ice cubes in his pocket?

He was trying to keep his cool.

Why couldn't the fans get soda pop at the double header?

Because the home team lost the opener.

Why don't baseball players join unions?

Because they don't like to be called out on strikes.

What is the difference between a baseball player and an angry musician?

One scores a hit, the other hits a score.

What is the difference between a sick cow and a crowd that doesn't like the umpire's decision?

One moos badly, the other boos madly.

What does a skunk do when it disagrees with the umpire?

It raises a stink.

• 6 •
TIME OUT

According to a new scientific theory, lifting weights kills germs. The only problem is getting the germs to lift weights.

Why do giants do push-ups every morning?
To get their extra-size (exercise).

When do people with colds get plenty of exercise?
When their noses run.

What is the difference between a boxer and a man with a cold?
A boxer knows his blows, a man with a cold blows his nose.

What medical problem helps you run faster?
Athlete's foot.

If athletes get athlete's foot, what do astronauts get?
Missile toe (mistletoe).

What has wheels and roars down the highway?
A lion on a skateboard.

What disease do racing cars get?
Vroom-atism.

DORIS: What does your mother do for a headache?

BORIS: She sends me out to play.

NELL: That nurse is in training.

DELL: Who is she going to fight?

When is heavy cream like a KO'd boxer?
When it is whipped and beaten.

BOXER (*in his corner*): Did I do him any damage?

TRAINER: No, but keep on swinging. The draft might give him a cold.

What happened when the nail had a fight with the tire?
The nail knocked it flat.

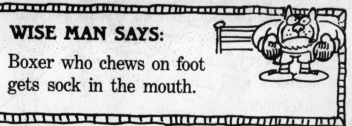

WISE MAN SAYS:

Boxer who chews on foot gets sock in the mouth.

What is the difference between a New Yorker and a dentist?
One roots for the Yanks, the other yanks for the roots.

DENTIST (*on the golf course, about to putt the ball into the hole*): Open wide!

What did the coach say when the whole team came down with the flu?

"*Win a flu, lose a flu.*"

WORLD'S WORST HEARTLESS DENTIST JOKE

The dentist was about to leave his office, golf bag on his shoulder, when the phone rang.

"Doctor," said the caller, "I have a terrible toothache. Can I stop by your office for a few minutes?"

"Sorry," replied the dentist, "I'm booked up. I have to fill 18 cavities this afternoon."

JILL: Say, how did you break your finger?
BILL: Playing football in a telephone booth.
JILL: What!
BILL: I was trying to get my quarterback.

"What impressed you most about the opposing team?" the reporter asked the losing football coach.

The coach shook his head, "The fact that when they ran onto the field, it tilted in their direction."

Why is measles like a football receiver?
Both are catching.

When are football receivers like judges?
When they sit on the bench.

MOTHER (*to sleeping son*): Sidney, it's twenty to eight!

SIDNEY (*still sleepy*): In whose favor?

FATHER: Now, Michael, don't be selfish. Let your sister have the sled half the time.

MICHAEL: I do, Dad. I have it going down the hill and she has it going up.

SUE: It's going to be tough sledding today.
DREW: Why is that?
SUE: No snow.

What do you need to play ice hockey?
Good ice sight (eyesight).

What winter sport do you learn in the fall?
Ice skating.

BETH: I fell down a dozen times while I was skating today. I was so embarrassed.
SETH: Why? Did anyone laugh at you?
BETH: Well, the ice cracked up!

Why did the cross country skier wear only one boot?
He heard the snow was one foot deep.

CLERK (*at ski lodge to registering guest*): Just your name, address and Blue Cross number, please.

What time is it when three skiers go ice skating and it begins to snow?
Wintertime.

Why did the ski pro say he was an actor?
*Because he broke his leg and was in a cast
for six months.*

What is a ski pro's favorite song?
"There's no business like snow business."

NIT: I played hockey last week and broke an
arm and a leg.
WIT: Some people get all the breaks!

TOMMY: I played soccer yesterday and sprained
my leg. That's why I was absent from
school.
TEACHER: Of all the lame excuses!

Why did the wrestler go to the psychiatrist?
He couldn't get a grip on himself.

Why did the fencer go to the psychiatrist?
Because of her duel (dual) personality.

PSYCHIATRIST: What did you dream about last night?
PATIENT: Baseball.
PSYCHIATRIST: Baseball—always baseball! Don't you ever dream about anything else?
PATIENT: What? And miss my turn at bat?

How did the cow feel when it struck out every time it came to bat?
Like an udder failure.

What is the difference between a slow ball and a fast ball?

The difference between a lump on the head and a fractured skull.

When was baseball first mentioned in the Bible?

In the opening words: "In the big inning (beginning). . . ."

In which inning is the score always 0–0?

In the OP-inning (opening).

What inning is it when the Frankenstein monster steps up to bat?

The fright-inning (frightening).

Why did the baseball team sign up a two-headed monster?

To play double-headers.

Why did the jogger go to the vet?

His calves hurt.

What did the jogger say when he ran into the vet's office?

"Ouch!"

What do joggers say when they leave you?

"So long—got to run!"

On Jeffrey's birthday, his parents bought him what he always wanted—a horse. But the horse didn't seem to have any energy. Jeffrey took it to the vet.

"This horse is very old," the vet said, after looking him over.

"Will I be able to race him?" asked Jeffrey.

The vet looked at Jeffrey and then he looked at the horse. "Sure," he said, "and you'll probably win."

Where do you take a sick race horse?
To the horse-pital.

Where do you take a sick pogo stick jumper?
To the hop-ital.

Where do you take a sick powerboat?
To the doc (dock).

Where do you take a sick hunting dog?
To the dog-ter.

• 7 •
RECORD BREAKERS

Did you hear about the Olympic athlete who jumped all over his Beatles album?

He was out to break a record.

Did you hear about the highest paid gymnast in the world?

She flew through the air with the greatest of fees.

Did you hear about the gymnast who looked at her bank book while she performed?

She wanted to check her balance.

What do you get if you cross a computer programmer and an Olympic athlete?

A floppy discus thrower.

What happened when the discus thrower lost the tournament?

He became discus-ted.

When does a broad jumper jump highest?

In a leap year.

Can any broad jumper jump higher than a house?

Yes, a house can't jump.

When can you jump over three men without getting up?

In a checkers game.

YOU: I bet I can jump across the street.
(When your friend says that you can't, walk across the street and jump.)

Dad was delighted to learn that his son had broken the school long-jump record.

"How did you do it, Son?" he asked.

"To tell the truth, Dad, I entered discus. But as I got ready to throw, I backed into a javelin."

What did the javelin say when it was thrown?

"Oh, spear me! Spear me!"

How do you make a cream puff?
Enter it in a marathon.

How do you make an egg run faster?
You egg it on.

Why was Adam the best runner of all time?
Because he was first in the human race.

SPORTS REPORTER: How do you feel about losing the race?

RUNNER: The agony of defeat (the feet).

What gets harder to catch the faster you run?
Your breath.

What animals always go with you when you jog?
Your calves.

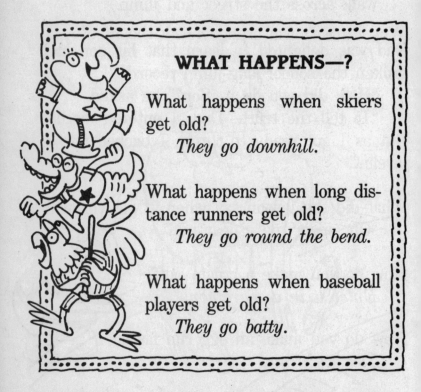

WHAT HAPPENS—?

What happens when skiers get old?
They go downhill.

What happens when long distance runners get old?
They go round the bend.

What happens when baseball players get old?
They go batty.

Which big punctuation mark is like a race?
A 40-yard dash.

Why does carrying a pencil always slow you down when you're running?
Because it is full of lead.

What kind of running means walking?
Running out of gas.

What did the athlete put in his sneakers to help him run faster?
Quicksand.

Why couldn't the orange finish the race?
It ran out of juice.

A cabbage, a faucet and a tomato had a race. How did it go?
The cabbage was ahead (a head), the faucet was running, and the tomato tried to ket-chup (catch up).

What race is like the Indianapolis 500—but without the apples?

The Indian apple-less 500.

Did you hear about the long-distance runner who took part in a 100-mile race? Well, he was in the lead and only had one more mile to go, but he was too tired to finish, so he turned around and ran back.

When are Olympic swimmers like babies?

When they do the crawl.

GOOD NEWS/BAD NEWS JOKE

At a championship high diving contest, a spectacular dive was performed to wild applause. Then the announcer's voice came over the loudspeaker:

"Ladies and gentlemen! I have some good news and some bad news. The good news is that the judges have awarded the magnificent dive you just witnessed a perfect score. The bad news is—there was no water in the pool."

CHIP: Did you hear the joke about the swan dive?

CHOP: No.

CHIP: That's swan on you!

Who is the best fencer in the ocean?
The swordfish.

GAME WARDEN: You fishing?

FISHERMAN: No, just drowning worms.

GAME WARDEN: Can't you read that sign? It says, "No Fishing Allowed!"

CAMPER: Oh, but I'm fishing silently.

What is the noisiest sport?

Tennis, because all the players raise a racket (racquet).

Why are fish poor tennis players?

They don't like to get close to the net.

BUMPER STICKER:

If you love tennis, HONK.
If you can't HONK, MAKE A RACKET!

Who was the first tennis player in history?

Joseph, in the Bible, because he served in Pharaoh's court.

What is the quietest sport?

Bowling, because you usually can hear a pin drop.

When is a bowling alley not on land or on water?

When it is on fire.

Why did all the bowling pins lie down?

They were on strike.

What can you do with old bowling balls?

Give them to elephants to shoot marbles with.

ROCK: You must be a great bowler.
JOCK: How did you know?
ROCK: I could tell by your pin head.

BING: You must be a great bowler.
BONG: How do you know?
BING: Your mind is always in the gutter.

Why do great bowlers play slowly?

Because they have time to spare.

Why is bowling good for teenagers?

Because it takes them off the streets and puts them in the alleys.

Did you ever see a salad bowl?
No, but I saw a fruit punch.

How do you make a fruit punch?
Give it boxing lessons.

What would you get if a rooster stepped into the ring with the heavyweight champion of the world?
Creamed chicken.

Why is boxing the world champion like singing in a barbershop quartet?
Because if you don't look sharp, you'll be flat.

DUFFY: When I was a sparring partner for the heavyweight champion, I gave him the biggest scare of his life.

MUFFY: *You* gave the champion a big scare?

DUFFY: Yes—he thought he killed me.

What happened when the watch fought the heavyweight champion of the world?

The watch took a licking, but kept on ticking.

WORLD'S SILLIEST MILKSHAKE JOKE

After ordering a milkshake, a man had to leave his seat in the restaurant to make a phone call. Since he didn't want anyone to take his drink, he took a paper napkin, wrote on it, "World's Strongest Weightlifter," and left it under his glass. When he returned from making his call, the glass was empty. Under it was a new napkin with new writing that said: "Thanks for the treat!" Signed, "The World's Fastest Runner."

How do mountain climbers hear?
With mountain ears (mountaineers).

WORLD'S DUMBEST MOUNTAIN CLIMBING JOKE

The two mountain climbers had reached the end of their exhausting journey. They were at the point of collapse, but they made it to the top. The first mountain climber turned to the other and said, "It almost cost us our lives to reach the top of this mountain and plant our country's flag, but it was worth it. This is the proudest moment of my life. Please—hand me the flag."

The second mountain climber stared at him in surprise and said, "I thought you brought it!"

What would you have to give up if you were the last person on earth?
Team sports.

• 8 •
WHO'S ON FIRST?

What song did the baseball player hum while he waited on third base?

"There's no place like home."

Harold came home from playing ball with tears streaming down his face. When his father asked him what was wrong, the little boy sobbed, "I was traded!"

"That shouldn't make you feel bad, Son. Even the greatest baseball players get traded."

"I know," replied Harold, "but I was traded for a torn glove!"

What is a personal foul?

A chicken you can call your own.

What famous ball player lived under a tree?

Babe Root (Ruth).

What is the difference between a boy who is late for dinner and a baseball hit over the fence?

One runs for home, the other is a home run.

LITTLE LEAGUE CATCHER: Can I take time out to clean my mask?

COACH: What happened?

LITTLE LEAGUE CATCHER: My bubble gum popped.

Why was the chef hired to coach the baseball team?

Because he knew how to handle a batter.

Why was the piano tuner hired to play on the baseball team?

Because he had perfect pitch.

LOU: A new pitcher is coming into the ball game.

PRU: That's a relief!

Which baseball league has the most trees and shrubs?

The bush leagues.

Where in a baseball stadium do the fans wear the whitest clothes?

In the bleachers.

What do executioners yell at a baseball game?

"Kill the umpire!"

What did the executioner say to the bowling pins?

"I'll spare you this time."

What did the executioner do at Christmas?

He went sleighing (slaying).

Out to Eat

What do bowlers order when they go into a restaurant?

Spare ribs.

What do basketball players order when they go into a restaurant?

Chicken in the basket.

What does an umpire do before he eats?

He brushes off his plate.

Why do fast-food lovers make good joggers?

Because they like to eat and run.

What do you have when cereals race?

Puffed wheat.

What do prize fighters bring to a picnic?

A box lunch.

What season is it when you're on a trampoline?

Springtime.

GEORGIE: I wish I had the money to buy a million golf balls.

PORGIE: What would you do with a million golf balls?

GEORGIE: Nothing. I just want the money.

Why is it so hard to drive a golf ball?
Because it doesn't have a steering wheel.

BARRY: Why don't you play golf with Jim anymore?

GARY: Would you play golf with a cheat who writes down the wrong score and moves the ball when you're not looking?

BARRY: No, I wouldn't.

GARY: Well, neither would he.

"Daddy," said the bright child who was accompanying her father in a round of golf, "why mustn't the ball go into the little hole?"

At breakfast on Sunday, Oscar suddenly announced that he had to go to the office.

"Listen," said Felix, "don't think you can just run off and play golf today and leave me here with all the chores."

"Golf!" protested Oscar, grabbing a piece of toast. "Golf is the furthest thing from my mind. Pass the putter!"

Man's Best Friend

What is a fighter's favorite dog?
A boxer.

What is a bowler's favorite dog?
A setter.

What is a weightlifter's favorite dog?
A Siberian husky.

What is a baseball player's favorite dog?
A good retriever that wears a muzzle, chases flies, and beats it for home when it sees the catcher.

What nationality are you when you run in a race?
Russian (rushin').

What nationality are you when you win a race?
Finnish (finish).

What runs but never gets out of breath?
Water.

What runs along with you and then lies under your bed with its tongue hanging out?
Your sneaker.

Why did the kind-hearted jogger wear ripple soles on his sneakers?
To give the ants a 50–50 chance.

Where do you go after you've jogged around a ship 10 times?
To the poop deck.

Why is a leaking faucet like a race horse?
It's off and running.

How would a vampire like to see a race finish?
Neck and neck.

What present does everyone kick about?
A soccer ball.

In ancient Greece the gods challenged the mortals to a game of soccer. The gods were surprised to see that one of the members of the mortals' team was half man and half horse.

"Who on earth is that?" asked Zeus.

"That," said the mortals' captain, "is our centaur forward."

FIRST CROCODILE: What is that funny-looking thing with two legs snorkling in the swamp?
SECOND CROCODILE: I don't know, but I'll bite!

YOU: I can stay under water for five minutes. (When the person you say this to tells you it is impossible, put a glass of water over your head and stand under it.)

Where do judges go to relax?
To the tennis court.

Where do nuclear scientists to go relax?
They go fission (fishin').

You know what fishing is? It's when a jerk on one end of the line waits for a jerk on the other.

LEM: How's the fishing around here?
CLEM: Fine.
LEM: Then how come you haven't caught anything?
CLEM: You asked me about the fishing, not the catching.

Why couldn't Batman go fishing?
Because Robin ate all the worms.

Did you hear about the silly camper who bought a sleeping bag? He spent three weeks trying to wake it up.

Where do little dogs sleep when they go camping?
In pup tents.

FATHER: Well, Son, you're back from your first camping trip. Did you fish with flies?

SON: Yes, Dad. I not only fished with them—I also camped with them, ate with them and slept with them.

Two flies were in the kitchen. Which one was the football player?
The one in the Sugar Bowl.

CUSTOMER: There's a fly swimming in my soup. What's he doing there?
WAITER: Looks like the backstroke to me.

CUSTOMER: Waiter, there's a fly in my soup?
WAITER: Yes, sir, and if you push over that pea, he'll play water polo.

COACH: Did you do your exercise this morning?
PLAYER: Sure thing, coach. I bent over and touched my sneakers 100 times.
COACH: You did?
PLAYER: Yes. Then I took them off the chair and put them on.

What is the difference between a girl who doesn't like her boyfriend and a surfer?
One is bored over a boy, and the other is a boy over a board.

What do you say to someone who falls off his surfboard because he's showing off?
"Surf's you right!"

• 9 •
YOU'RE PUTTING ME ON!

A lemon and an orange were on a high diving board. The orange jumped, but the lemon didn't. Why?

The lemon was yellow.

AMELIA: Would you like to see me dive off that high diving board?

DELIA: Yes.

AMELIA: And I thought you were a friend of mine!

What is the soft, mushy stuff between a shark's teeth?

Slow swimmers.

What is a frightened scuba diver?
Chicken of the Sea.

How do moths swim?
They do the butterfly.

What is the only way a miser will swim?
Freestyle.

Is it better to swim on a full or on an empty stomach?
Neither. It's better to swim on water.

What do you say when you swim into kelp and it pulls you down?

"*Kelp!*"

DROWNING MAN: Help! Help!
PASSERBY: What's the matter?
DROWNING MAN: I can't swim!
PASSERBY: So what? I can't play golf—but I don't go around shouting about it!

SWIMMING INSTRUCTOR: What is the first step in saving a drowning person?
BOY SCOUT: Take him out of the water.
SWIMMING INSTRUCTOR: Good. Now what is the second step?
BOY SCOUT: Take the water out of him.

GOOD NEWS/BAD NEWS JOKE

SLAVEMASTER (*to Roman galley slaves who have been pulling on the oars for hours*): I have some good news and some bad news. The good news is that you can have a 15-minute rest. The bad news is that at the end of the rest period, the captain wants to go waterskiing.

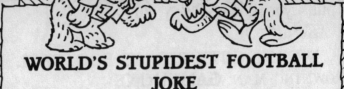

WORLD'S STUPIDEST FOOTBALL JOKE

"Okay, Smith," said the coach, "get in there and tackle 'em!"

Smith went into the game. Soon the opposing team was doubled over with laughter. The game had to be stopped.

"What are you doing?" asked the coach. "Why aren't you tackling the other team?"

"Oh—tackle!" said Smith. "I thought you said tickle!"

Why did the football coach date the watch?
He wanted to take time out.

Why couldn't the football player make a phone call?
He couldn't find the receiver.

MOTHER MONSTER: Why don't you play football with your little brother?

LITTLE MONSTER: Aw, mom. I'd much rather have a real football to kick around.

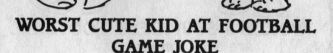

WORST CUTE KID AT FOOTBALL GAME JOKE

A man and his four-year-old son were watching a professional football game on TV. After a bad play, the father exploded:

"Just look at that stupid halfback. He fumbles three times, and every time the other team recovers! Why do they let someone like that play in the game?"

The little boy thought it over. "Daddy," he said, "maybe it's his ball."

Why did the silly athlete bring a rod and reel to the football tryouts?

He heard they were looking for a tackle.

What kitten do you need when a football team tackles you?

A first-aid kit.

What do you get when a football team plays in your potato field?

Mashed potatoes.

What can you serve, but never eat?
A tennis ball.

JAN: Will you join me in a game of tennis?
DAN: Why, are you coming apart?

How does a tennis player sneeze?
"A-tennis-shoe! A-tennis-shoe!"

Why is tennis such a romantic sport?
Because every game starts with "love."

What do you call a Czech whose tennis match
is called off?
A cancelled Czech (check).

What goes, "gnip-gnop, gnip-gnop?"
A Ping-Pong ball bouncing backwards.

How do you slice a Ping-Pong ball?
With a knife.

What do you do to a bad Ping-Pong ball?
Paddle it.

WISE MAN SAYS:

Never play Ping-Pong
with open mouth.

Why is Count Dracula like the Frankenstein monster?
> *Neither can play Ping-Pong.*

Why didn't the cow want to play Ping Pong?
> *She wasn't in the moo-d.*

Did you ever see the wood fence?
> No, but I saw the barn dance.

MORE DANCING

Where do bugs dance?
> *At the fly ball.*

Where do groceries dance?
> *At the basketball.*

Where do skiers dance?
> *At the snowball.*

Where do caddies dance?
> *At the golf ball.*

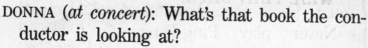

DONNA (*at concert*): What's that book the conductor is looking at?

LANA: That's the score!

DONNA: Really? Who's winning?

VICKIE: My father can hold up ten cars and a truck.

NICKIE: He must be the world's greatest weightlifter.

VICKIE: No, he's a traffic cop.

FLAP: My brother was doing all right until they caught up with him.

JACK: I didn't know your brother was a crook.

FLAP: He isn't. He's a race car driver.

What musical key do you hear when a race car speeds through a coal mine?

A-flat miner (minor).

What musical instruments are best for catching fish?

Castanets.

GAME WARDEN: Don't you know you can't fish without a permit?

BOY: That's all right, mister. I'm doing fine with these worms.

A fisherman tried several different kinds of bait without getting a single bite. Finally, in disgust, he threw a handful of coins into the lake.

"Okay, wise guys!" he shouted to the fish. "Go out and buy something you like!"

Clem and Lem were fishing. For three hours neither of them moved a muscle. Then Lem shifted his foot a couple of times. Clem grumbled: "That's the second time you've moved your foot in 20 minutes. Did you come here to fish or to dance?"

MOST IRRITATING CUTE KID FISHING JOKE

Little Doris, aged four, was fishing with her father, who was wearing his fishing license on the back of his hat. They weren't having any luck.

"Daddy," Little Doris said, "turn your hat around so the fish can see your license."

GAME WARDEN: Catch any fish?

FISHERMAN: Did I! I took out forty this morning!

GAME WARDEN: That's illegal. Know who I am? I'm the game warden.

FISHERMAN: Know who I am? I'm the biggest liar in the world.

DALE: Today is the big game. I'm so nervous—
I have butterflies in my stomach.

GALE: Why don't you take aspirins?

DALE: I did. The butterflies are playing croquet with them.

How do witches feel when they play croquet?
Wicket.

What has two wings but doesn't fly?
A hockey team.

What happens when a hockey player tastes a
lemon?
He puckers up.

"Are you ready out there in radio land for your morning exercises? Good. Now—up, down, up, down, up, down. Now the other eyelid."

DID YOU HEAR—?

Did you hear about the boxer who couldn't find anything to drink? Someone beat him to the punch.

Why did the monster give up boxing?
He didn't want to improve his looks.

What do you call it when a weightlifter drops his dumbbell?
A power failure.

What happened when the weightlifter took a bath?
The police made him bring it back.

What shellfish lift weights?
Mussels (muscles).

STAN: Did you hear about the mean wrestler who was pretty and ugly at the same time?
NAN: How could that be?
STAN: Well, he was pretty ugly.

What would you get if a pig learned karate?
Pork chops.

"Mom, can I go out and play baseball?"
"With those holes in your socks?"
"No, with the kids next door."

CHILD (*at first baseball game*): Daddy, why is that man running?
FATHER: Because he hit the ball.
CHILD: Is he afraid it's going to hit him back?

What kind of hit do you find in the zoo?
A lion (line) drive.

Have you ever seen a line drive?
No, but I've seen a ball park.

What insect is found in the grass of a ball park?

A ground fly.

Why can't turtles play baseball?

They can't run home.

What do you give to a bird who crashes into a fly ball?

First aid tweetment.

Which takes longer to run: First to second base? Or second to third base?

Second to third base, because there is a shortstop in the middle.

What is the biggest diamond in the world?

A baseball field.

Why is a baseball field hot after the game?

Because all the fans have gone home.

What would you get if Mickey Mantle married Betty Crocker?

Better batters.

What is the difference between a rain barrel and a bad fielder?

One catches drops, the other drops catches.

DUSTY: Mom, I can't find my baseball glove.

MOTHER: Did you look in the car?

DUSTY: Where in the car?

MOTHER: Try the glove compartment.

Little Arnold was pitching for the Little League team. After he walked the first six players that came up, he was taken out of the game.

"It isn't fair!" he moaned. "I was pitching a no-hitter!"

RITCHIE (*at baseball game*): Can I give money to that man who's crying?

FATHER: That's very kind of you, Son. What's he crying about?

RITCHIE: "Hot dogs! Peanuts! Popcorn!"

Where do they put crying children?
   In the bawl (ball) park.

NEIGHBOR: I heard your child bawling last night.

FATHER: Yes, and after four bawls, he got his base warmed.

TOM: What small dog do you find in a ball park?

JERRY: A hot dog?

TOM: No, pup corn.

Baseball Jokes You Don't Want to Hear

Did you hear the joke about the fast pitch?

Never mind, you just missed it.

Did you hear the joke about the pop fly?

Never mind, it's way over your head.

Did you hear the joke about the Most Valuable Player award?

Never mind, you wouldn't get it.

Did you hear the joke about your pitching style?

Never mind, it's foul.

Did you hear the joke about the baseball?

No, how does it go?

It doesn't go. You have to throw it.

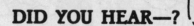

DID YOU HEAR—?

Did you hear about the basketball player who was on television? His mother made him get off.

Did you hear about the baseball team that was so rich, all its bases were loaded?

Why are basketball players tall?
Because their heads are so far from their feet.

How do very tall basketball players greet each other?
They say, "Small world, isn't it?"

Why did the basketball player wear his watch on his ankle?
He wanted to play overtime.

CHICK: You play one-on-one basketball with your dog? He must be very unusual.
RICK: Not really. I beat him most of the time.

• 10 •
TAKE THAT!

DIT: Your mother and father must have lifted weights.

DOT: What makes you say that?

DIT: How else could they have raised a big dumbbell like you?

Let's see what kind of athlete you are. How about holding your breath for ten minutes?

GLADYS: I'm going to the blood bank.

MERVYN: Don't bother. They need plasma, not asthma.

Before you decide to be a blood donor—make sure you're a blood owner.

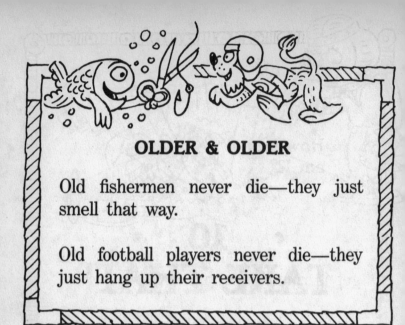

OLDER & OLDER

Old fishermen never die—they just smell that way.

Old football players never die—they just hang up their receivers.

GILLY: I know someone who is so dumb, he lost $20 betting on a football game.

DILLY: What's so dumb about that?

GILLY: Well, he lost $10 betting on the play—the other $10 on the instant replay.

Melvin was playing football very badly. He tried to kick a goal and missed. Finally, he threw himself down on the bench and said in disgust, "Boy, I could kick myself!"

The coach looked the other way. "Don't bother," he said, "you'd probably miss."

NIP: You'd make a great football player.

TUCK: Really?

NIP: Yes—even your breath is offensive.

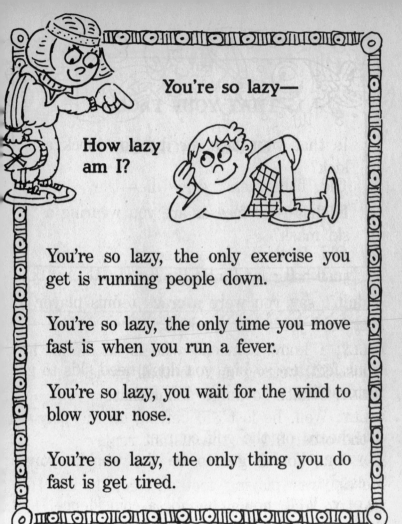

You're so lazy—

How lazy am I?

You're so lazy, the only exercise you get is running people down.

You're so lazy, the only time you move fast is when you run a fever.

You're so lazy, you wait for the wind to blow your nose.

You're so lazy, the only thing you do fast is get tired.

"I don't know what's the matter with me today," said the baseball player, as he struck out several times in a row. "I'm not playing my usual game."

"Oh" said the coach sarcastically, "What game is that?"

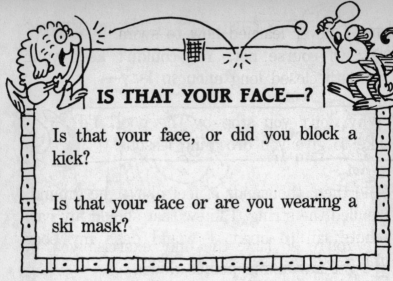

IS THAT YOUR FACE—?

Is that your face, or did you block a kick?

Is that your face or are you wearing a ski mask?

I didn't say you were a crack tennis player. I just said you were cracked.

Your feet are so big, you don't need skis to go waterskiing.

Overheard on the golf course:
GOLFER: You've got to be the world's worst caddy.
CADDY: Well, how's that for a coincidence!

PAT: I'm on my way to try out for the school swimming team.
RAT: Are you joking? You can barely fight the current when you let out the bath water!

ELLA: I can swim with my head above water.
DELLA: Of course, wood floats, right?

STU: I never learned how to swim.

SUE: Of course not. You couldn't keep your mouth closed long enough.

Why don't you stop by the pool? I'd like to give you drowning lessons.

"And then, thousands of feet above the ground, I pulled the string. I knew that should my parachute fail to open, I would dash my poor brains out on the ground below."

"And—did you?"

CANDY: The national sport in Spain is bull fighting and in England it's cricket.

MANDY: I'd rather play in England.

CANDY: Why?

MANDY: I'd rather fight crickets.

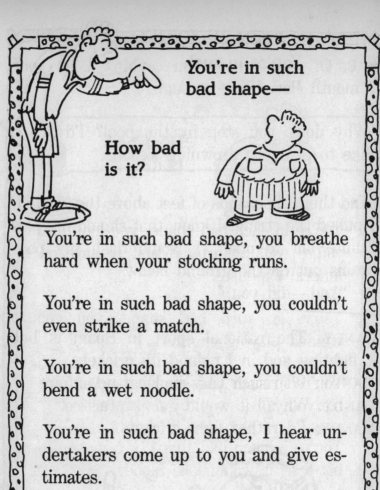

You're in such bad shape—

How bad is it?

You're in such bad shape, you breathe hard when your stocking runs.

You're in such bad shape, you couldn't even strike a match.

You're in such bad shape, you couldn't bend a wet noodle.

You're in such bad shape, I hear undertakers come up to you and give estimates.

You're in such bad shape, you couldn't even beat a rug.

If your body were a building, it would be condemned.

You're in shape, all right—the wrong shape.

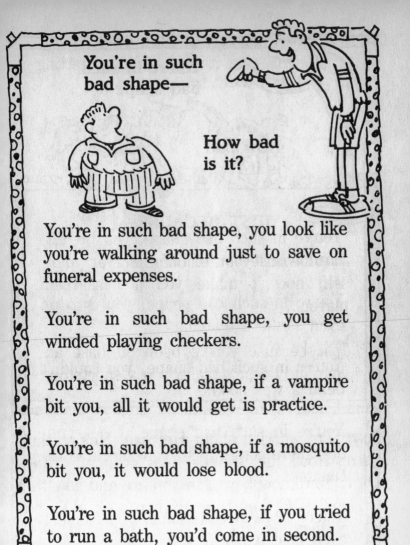

You're in such bad shape—

How bad is it?

You're in such bad shape, you look like you're walking around just to save on funeral expenses.

You're in such bad shape, you get winded playing checkers.

You're in such bad shape, if a vampire bit you, all it would get is practice.

You're in such bad shape, if a mosquito bit you, it would lose blood.

You're in such bad shape, if you tried to run a bath, you'd come in second.

Your shape isn't half bad—it's all bad.

GIG: I can bend bars with my bare hands.
WIG: Sure, chocolate bars.

BIFF: I have the body of an athlete.

CLIFF: Better give it back. You're getting it out of shape.

JUST BECAUSE—

Just because you dribble all over yourself, doesn't make you a basketball player.

Just because you've been off base all your life doesn't make you a shortstop.

TOOT: I'm worried about Herman. He's so thin.

COOT: How thin is he?

TOOT: You know how thin you are and how thin I am? Well, he's thinner than both of us put together.

YIP: I was great in sports when I was young. I had the body of an athlete.

YAP: Well, you still have the feet.

Some people can tear a telephone book in two. You'd have trouble with a wet Kleenex tissue.

You're so weak—

How weak and I?

You're so weak, you couldn't even lick a lollipop.

You're so weak, you would have trouble beating a drum.

You're so weak, you couldn't even crack a joke.

You're so weak, you couldn't even carry a tune.

You're so weak, if you played a piano, the piano would win.

You're so weak, if you beat an egg, we'd all be surprised.

DID YOU HEAR—?

Did you hear about the athlete who tried out for the track team?
   He couldn't even jump to a conclusion.

Did you hear about the athlete who tried out for the pole vault?
   He could barely clear his throat.

You remind me of a relief pitcher. If I don't have to look at you—it's a relief.

You remind me of a racquetball game—you're off the wall.

That uniform fits you like a glove—a boxing glove.

My doctor told me to exercise with dumbbells. Care to join me in the gym?

• 11 •
GIVE UP?

Why did the chicken cross the football field?
To score a touchdown.

Why did the surfer cross the ocean?
To get to the other tide.

Why did the otter cross the playground?
To get to the otter slide.

Why did the hen sit down in the middle of the tennis court?
She wanted to lay it on the line.

What serious crime would you get arrested for anywhere except in a ball park?
Hit-and-run.

Where do great dragon baseball players go?
To the Hall of Flame.

SHOPPER (*in sports shop*): May I have a baseball glove for my son?

CLERK: Sorry, madam, we don't swap.

STANLEY: We played baseball in school today and I stole second base.

MOTHER: Well, you march right over to school and give it back!

FATHER: I hear you played hookey from school today to play baseball.

SON: No, Dad, and I have the fish to prove it.

What is the best way to reach a fish?
Drop him a line.

TIP: I was down at the lake and I saw a cat-fish.

TOP: Really? How did it hold the rod?

Homer agreed to take care of his little sister Suzy while his parents went shopping. He asked if he could take her fishing, and they said it was all right.

"I'll never take her fishing with me again," Homer complained to his parents when they got home. "I didn't catch a single fish."

"I'm sure she'll be quiet next time," his mother said. "Just explain that the fish swim away when there's noise."

"It wasn't the noise," Homer said. "She ate the bait!"

A brother and sister went to the seashore for the first time. On seeing the ocean, the little boy said, "Look at all that water!"

The little girl thought for a moment and said, "Yes, and that's only the top."

FIRST FISHERMAN: Is this a good lake for fish?

SECOND FISHERMAN: It must be terrific. I can't get any of them to come out.

SHOPPER: I'm going on a fishing trip, and I'd like to buy some tackle. Please hurry—I have to catch a bus.

CLERK: I'm sorry, sir, we don't have fishing tackle that big.

Marvin had been fishing all day without luck. On his way home, he stopped into a fish market and said to the clerk, "Please stand there and throw me a few of your biggest trout."

The clerk was puzzled. "Throw them to you? What for?"

"I may be a poor fisherman," Marvin replied, "but I'm no liar. I want to be able to say I caught them myself!"

Four-year-old Jeannie, visiting her aunt's summer cottage, was watching a couple of water-skiers on the lake. Turning to her aunt, she said, "Those men are so dumb! They're never going to catch up with that boat!"

What is brown, hairy and attached to the back of a boat?

An outboard coconut.

DID YOU HEAR—?

Did you hear the joke about the man who went deep-sea fishing?

Never mind, you can't fathom it.

Did you hear the joke about the slippery fish?

Never mind, you won't catch on.

"Are you the wonderfully brave young man who tried to save my son's life when he broke through the ice on the lake?"

"Yes, ma'am."

"Well—where did you hide his mittens?"

FLIP: I've been swimming since I was five years old.

FLOP: Gosh, you must be tired!

CINDY: Swimming is the best exercise for keeping your body slim and beautiful.

WINDY: Oh, yeah? Did you ever look at a duck?

CAL: Do you know the difference between an old baseball glove and a piece of candy?

VAL: No.

CAL: Good, then eat this old baseball glove and give me that piece of candy.

FATHER: Son, you've struck out so many times with the bases loaded in the Little League playoffs, I might have to do something I don't want to do.

JUNIOR: What's that, Dad?

FATHER: I may have to trade you.

Why didn't the Confederate soldier want to go to the ball game?

Because he heard the Yankees were playing.

Why did the Confederate baseball player get so little pay?

He didn't belong to the Union.

Did you hear about the baseball game between the "Collars" and the "Shirts"?

The game ended in a tie.

Why did the pitcher let the baseball player walk?

He was too tired to run.

What do you get if you cross a pitcher and the Invisible Man?

Pitching like no one has ever seen.

LITTLE BILLY (*looking at a catcher's mask*): Why do they make that man wear a mask?

LITTLE LILY: Maybe it keeps him from biting the other players.

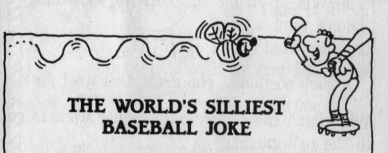

THE WORLD'S SILLIEST BASEBALL JOKE

A professional baseball player was walking along the street one day when, to his horror, he saw a baby about to fall from a window. He dashed to the building and caught the baby, who was saved—unhurt. However, the force of the habit proved too much for him. Without realizing what he was doing, he straightened up and threw the baby to first base.

How are song writers like baseball players?

They're both interested in big hits.

That weightlifter is so tough—

How tough is she?

She's so tough, she uses steel wool for a powder puff.

She's so tough, she uses a pickax to part her hair.

She's so tough, she gargles with Drano.

She's so tough, she uses industrial strength perfume.

WEIGHTLIFTER: I can lift an elephant with one hand.

ROGER: I don't believe you.

WEIGHTLIFTER: Okay, bring me an elephant with one hand and I'll prove it.

What has 22 legs and goes, "Crunch, crunch, crunch"?

A football team eating potato chips.

What happens when an egg sees a thrilling football game?

It gets egg-cited.

COACH: Elmer, you can be the end, guard and tackle.

ELMER: That's great, coach!

COACH: Yes, sit at the *end* of the bench, *guard* the water bucket, and *tackle* anyone who gets near it.

THE WORLD'S WORST TALKING DOG JOKE

Walking down the street, a man was stopped by someone who wanted to sell a talking dog for ten dollars.

The man couldn't believe his ears when the dog said, "Please buy me. I'm really a great dog. I played professional football. One year I was even nominated the most valuable player."

"That dog really does talk!" gasped the man, amazed. "But why in the world would you want to sell him for only ten dollars?"

"I can't stand liars," said the dog's owner. "He never played professional football."

PIT: I met someone who is so dumb, he thinks a football coach has four wheels.

PAT: How many wheels does it have?

TONY: I'm no longer the quarterback on our team.

BONY: What happened?

TONY: It's all my mother's fault. She made me promise not to pass anything until somebody said, "Please."

Why did the silly kid bring a ladder to the ball game?

He wanted to shake hands with the Giants.

NUT: Are you a Giant fan?

TUT: Yes.

NUT: Well, I'm a little air conditioner myself.

COACH: What this team needs is life!

MANAGER: Aw, coach, don't you think thirty days is enough?

FATHER: Well, son, did you make the school football team?

SON: I'm not sure, Dad. The coach took one look at me and said, "This is the end!"

INDEX